Hard Landing

By **Rick Smith**

LUMMOX Press

ISBN 978-1-929878-89-5

Lummox Press
PO Box 5301
San Pedro, CA 90733

www.lummoxpress.com

Printed in the United States of America.

Our thanks to the editors of the following journals and
publications where some of these poems have previously
appeared: Bachy; Blueline; Friends of Acadia Magazine; Hanging
Loose; Heron Dance; Into the Teeth of the Wind; Latitamba;
The Lummox Journal; Nexus; Water~Stone; 88; The Long Way
Home (The Little Red Book anthology, Lummox Press); Eyes Like
Mingus (jazz poetry anthology, Lummox Press); Stonecloud
(post card series). Thirty-four of these poems were published
in The Wren Notebook (Lummox Press, 2000).

Cover art by RD Armstrong
Back cover painting by Ferol Smith, photo by Bernard Van Leer

A special thanks to the following who have inspired, encouraged and assisted with this work:

Aesop; John Lyon; Chris "Wren Noir" Yeseta; to the illustrators— Judith Bever, Bonnie Love-Nordoff, and RD Armstrong; Angela Copple; Lorrine Parks; Pastor Jim Coen; Vicki Lindner; Sharon West; Mira Nakashima; George Nakashima; Clabe Hangan; Deborah Clark Yeseta; Steve and Melani Wysocki; Barry Gifford; Phil Daughtry; Victoria Chang; Kathleen Norris; Leonard Cohen; Tu Fu; Charles Simic; Kathlin Smith; R. Kim Smith; Mom Smith; Mom Latessa; Julia Sweeney; Jessica Nordoff; my wife Erika, for enduring each draft; Steve (bottom dog) Armstrong, for pushing the river. And finally, in loving memory of Sara Ellen Wold McGimsey.

A CD of Rick Smith reading

these poems was recorded

by John Lyon in 2009

and 2010 at Alta Loma

Psychological Associates

in Rancho Cucamonga,

California, and is available

through Lummox Press.

Introduction to the Wren Poems ›››

I met Rick Smith in a Dante class, Bard College, circa 1965. He revolved in, six feet four, as if his boots were made out of wheels. Tattered elbows, wing-like, poked the walls. He pushed his bright flap of hair off his one good eye, bloodshot now—an owl who'd cried Huuu huh u Huu! all night. But not a wren.

He played harp with "The Disciples," he said. A naïve girl, I imagined him plucking a curved gold instrument, like Allen Ginsberg's naked angel. When I went "down the road" to hear the group, I saw the harmonica buried between his fist and lips. He produced an insistent bluesy wail with it, but I saw him as a Red Tailed Hawk, cruising silently alert above. Hardly a tiny creeping wren.

Luckily he admired me, because few did. A hopeful scholar, I burrowed into library stacks, while Rick morphed from bird to bird, sometimes a fierce-beaked speedy falcon, then a stranded eagle, looking out for territory, feathers raked by violent winds. He told me once that, as a child, he'd lost his mother. I should have known: the giant stride, the hungry voice concealed a delicate unfledged baby wren.

Forty-five years ago, we became friends, the careful duck and Great Blue Heron, zooming down the rushing river. Rick worked summers in a bloody rendering plant to pay tuition. He drove cross country, four days straight, to connect with L.A. music vibes, and an extravagantly beautiful theatrical girl-friend. A one-man V of migrating geese, he was nothing like a secretive, observant wren.

When he lived in California, and I in New York, we wrote letters. I still have them. From every envelope burst a poem. Not about wrens. He wrote all the time, songs, lyrics, like my child-hood canary, who trilled his heart out, just because the sun shone, and he hadn't molted. Rick lived in a tiny cottage with a gate back then, sold candy on the street to pay the rent.

For a short time, (and this will embarrass him), we thought we'd be lovers. Great idea! Flocks of poems flew between us. But when I arrived at LAX, wearing a buttercup knit mini-dress, he wasn't there. His old car had blown a tire on the freeway— signaling that some things break so they can live. When he finally showed up, a long time later, he was covered with oil, like a Sea Gull caught in Exxon's Valdez spill. No damned Wren!

But birds of a feather stick together, even as the glaciers melt. Gradually we begin talking and writing again, spend one weird New Year's Eve in frigid New York City. In the years to come, my friend becomes a shrink—who would believe it? He still plays harp with The Hangan Bros and Mescal Sheiks. He sends the discs. He writes poems, fervently now, makes records, performs in clubs, all while treating brain-injured people. He finally marries Erika (happily) and produces Saunder, an interesting son—a miracle!

And his poetry? Still drifting in with every letter, it expands in skill and intimate affect. The first volume, *The Wren Notebook*, reveals a large, inquiring spirit, paying homage to the infinite metaphors in a single phenomenon. "The wren lends itself to ethical and etymological inquiry," the poet says. This new collection, including lyrics from volume one, plus new poems, embodies an expansive, precise, obdurate rhythm, a generous wisdom and tender vision. This is the mature Rick Smith, delving deeper into what is smaller.

Vicki Lindner
Denver, Colorado
March, 2010

Vicki Lindner is an award-winning fiction writer, essayist, and journalist. She is an Associate Professor Emerita at the University of Wyoming and on the faculty of Lighthouse Writers in Denver.

Table of Contents ›››

Hard
Landing

Judith Bever

(for Clabe Hangan)

Wren shudders
as usual
upon awakening.

That part about
heaven and earth…

Sky is something
she can't touch
but it's home.

And the dangers of a land
she can dig her beak into
give her fits.

Now, 70 feet above the L.A. River
her place in the sky
is transparent.

No tracks,
no sign.
Only hearsay evidence
she touched this air.

The invisibility
is near perfect.

A picture window
she climbs through.

Place a twig among
unborn Wrens
and the mother
will feel the need
to destroy the nest
and fly into the ocean
which is not her home.

These wings they make me crazy
I don't sleep, I can't stop.
Sleep is not a destination it is
the distance
between lives.

(Walking With My Mom, Toledo, 1947)

Plain, brown, small,
set apart by a musical scream,
wren fits in,
speechless in a way
but always in private harmony,
always with mad motion
and hard to accompany,
key of C# minor.

There is a wall
at the entrance
to the Cherry Street Bar & Grill.
One final glass brick slides in
like a sound installation
and mom is picking me up.
I notice the brick
because now the wall is complete.
It's a wall you can nearly see through,
vague brown shapes
move fast and look wavy
on the other side.

That's what I remember.
That and walking out of there
holding my mom's hand.
She's saying, "You probably
won't remember this moment."

When we look up,
there are geese,
like alphabet parts and numbers vibrating
in the sky, Mom says,
"Geese can change everything.
They sing in horn keys."

How did she know
that was just
what I was thinking?

I write what I can remember. I make notes, keep notebooks. I wake up and start writing. Sense of direction abandons me. Wrong turns, avoidable delays, instructions from strangers. I'm lost on the Delaware by Ringing Rocks, Upper Black Eddy; looking for Half Moon Bay and turning circles over Lisbon. In sleep, it is gravity which fails me. I remember parts of the dream:

the broken window
the red dirt
the orange moon pressing shamelessly
against the lighthouse,
the lighthouse going up in flame,
falling into Half Moon Bay.

Wren hears the music before he is born. It is inside the wood, the rocks, the fiber. The music is in predawn Wren; it betrays his hiding place among the branches of a nightshade plant over the loading dock. It is 1894, Half Moon Lighthouse: the cat and the Wren go up in flame (or) the cat eats the Wren. Something like that. I have no idea what it means when the moon rises orange and full and lingers like it does. But the light enters Wren as the energy of fire closes in on the sea.

We are not viola da gamba,
kettle drum, trumpet.
We are piccolo, fife,
nose flute, pan pipe.
We accompany thunder.
We are troglodytidae:

cave, hole, bra-on-the-line,
sock dwellers,
primitive and deep
in the pocket. We could
never
sleep until noon. Not with so
many wings moving.

But what does the wind seek
when it flirts with shallow water
or makes magnolia leaves
slap like polite applause
when beauty crashes to earth.

The slope & line of our
horizon is
perfect pitch and
the explosions are always
in the distance except for
the last one.

(for John Forsha)

Something is going on
in the north of Spain
and winging over the Guggenheim,
I'm so incredibly brown
it would help to be color blind.
Something about spring:
it's a trick
to nest in a building
made of titanium.
And the action:
rendez-vous et tête-a-tête,
the tourists and the Basques,
dreaming up improvisations,
scribbling on paper plates
between crumbs & jam and
not sure what it means. Everybody pretending
not to speak French

Below:
it's as simple as it seems
and it never seems that simple,
imagining scenes,
we become exactly what
we are,
especially at dawn
when the outlines
take on detail
and new heat is suggested.

A man on crutches
walks over cobblestone:
crutches and a bêret,
dressed for winter.

Do you see what I mean?

Reyezuelo, roitelet, little king, gold crested
wren. Wren, reina.
86 A.D.: Wren
stowing beneath Eagle's great wings,
taking off fresh at 12,000 feet
to break for the sky.
Does that make for royalty?

The runaway truck ramp is closed again
coming down the 15 past Cajon.
This would be the wrong night
to lose the brakes.
But the fog hugs me,
holds my shaking like Mom
while the jazz station
out of Redlands
seems to go mad with intrusion,
an overload of signal,
before it breaks up.

These birds up here, they can't agree on anything.
Altitude, standards of conduct, rules of engagement,
the territorial imperatives. Solos are border
skirmishes and circuit breakers as common ground
slips into grey. So how did Wren, short distance
flyer of the first order, make his bones up here?
What's left of his reputation is rubble. Of course,
he's a damn King in Spain. But that's Spain, holding
to Spanish logic in a land where nothing is obvious.

En route from Bilbao to Paris, Wren curses the
Pyrenees well past Bordeaux. He has "no comment"
on his ancient debt. But the unforgiving eagle,
burdened with a memory for motive, takes the
opportunity... "In the old days, he just couldn't get
enough of me, but now I know, it just takes fog and
a little deception to get where he's going."

Increasingly, I'm able
to ignore poor visibility,
the smell of brake lining,
bad radio,
long odds
and the nearby whistle of two hawks,
one black, one red,
who have learned the fundamentals
of treachery.

There is danger in everything we
want.

Wren is a shadow of a bird
who is not afraid to take a ride.
She is privileged
to pass this afternoon
inspecting the ruined coastal towers
of Madagascar
from the back
of a Sea Eagle.

For a moment
Wren is lost
in a cloud.

(The largest wren in
North America is
the Cactus Wren.)
A small spotted owl
looks like a big brother
and plays a deadly hide-and-seek
but the owl cannot follow
where the cactus wren
flies with ease:
Try concentrating on the tail
and follow the flutter
with that wide angle iris
tilting like a satellite dish
that can pick up Ethiopia;
you come up short.
You cannot climb through
the sea of thorns I put
between us.

Try concentrating on the silence
of the night.

Sometimes silence is
just silence.
But there is none here.

RD Armstrong

Faultlines & bloodlines
run deep. They are,
simply,
what they are:
in place
even through these puzzle clouds
and turtles in the sky.

If you watch from above,
some boundaries are different.
Frontiers and datelines
are inventions,
theory, not really
of this earth.
They are, simply,
not there, even
through these puzzle clouds
and turtles
in the sky.

(for Gary Winkel)

Crash landings and small craft warnings
seeds and grasses in
the crosswind of the plains.
This defiance is perilous:
darting in and out,
a ground skirmish
with a young buffalo, the size of a continent,
who seems not to notice
but who avoids stepping on any of us.

Huge and tiny
everywhere,
nowhere.

The wind is a street gang
on the west end of Dakota.
It blows us so hard, we
cannot recover. It blows us
flat, blows us
like darts sideways
into barns, south if we're lucky
but then, we need permission
to leave. We are expelled
yet we are charged with
abandonment. We are
at large.
There is no easy passage
on the west end of Dakota.

Wren loses his place
in the wires.
You know how they smile
their wren smiles
when they dive.

To lose footing and smile,
that's the way it is
up in the air.

(for Mom Smith)

Wren on ash,
wren on birch,
spots on the skin,
the character of a
wren on saguaro,
on palm, in light
in blue and black,
on curved wall, on brick.
Wren on rock & wood,
in snow, straw, sand. The
shape of small boats,
sliding on water, followed
by gulls. And, bone to bone;
ossicles, wired, they chime.
On wind.

Bonnie Love-Nordoff

Landing on the right place
the breath takes on a
rhythm and
i can't see my feet
the branch approaches
the vision narrows in and
the feet are where
they need to be
i'm not trapped by this
shape
and the sun is good today.

(for Mama Latessa)

It's about heat and rhythm
this little heart pounding
to the limit an alarm
clock at the crack of dawn.
Wren does not fly that straight
but this time
it's a beeline close
enough to straight.
There is really no need for straight lines.
It's about heat and rhythm.

There is thirst
and there is fear
both precise
so precise that
there is no more dawn
no more trees
no more endless curved space
wrapped around the horizon
like passion
and drinking deep is cut short
with the swiveling, the scanning
for cat and kestrel.

There is thirst
and there is fear
and there is always one tiny
hole waiting for you
to fill.

Marsh Wren has this habit:
I build, I build, I build and
I build but it is
all display.
I do not pause to organize
these constructions.
There is no pausing
but I do get excited
and fear sneaks away
it disappears so well
I cannot even remember
its smell.

And I stay busy
letting humanity pass
like a shadow,
keeping it at a distance but
still close enough so as not to draw attention.

And who will it be
to finally build that place
where
I can settle
where I do not pause
to organize
these constructions.

The Marsh Wren,
the wren
with explosions
in his head,
the wren who will
look into the reflection,
drink deep
and pretend
not to pretend.

Rock Wren is not a hard little bird;
she suffers in the cold
and has to winter
in the tumbled slate
on Three Kings Mountain.
She sleep in fits.
The dream is always the same:

the sun
the cold river.

I can tell they're working and
it must be something important
because it's Flag Day
and all the lights are on.
I can feel movement
it's the steady rhythm
of something outside me.
And then we go down and down
further than any wren has ever been
and darkness crushes me.
My own rib cage is
the last line of defense
and they've gotten past it
by replicating it with
something outside me.
They're going into the mines
and they're all out of canaries.
I'm swinging from some carpus and
from my perch in this cage
within a cage
going down
on a one way
incense loaded sleep.

Wings folded, eyes unblinking
a little fascinated
a little cold.

Cold makes me die.

In my mind, I'm flying
on the edge of sorrow
but I can outrun that cloud.
I can break out of this cage,
crack this mind body equation.
I can look into
that little round mirror
with the blue plastic frame
and reassure myself.

"You Are My Sunshine"
floats through my head.

Oh, it's going to be a long night.

Judith Bever

A splash of orange
slanders a black sky
and the wren heads for cover.
The wren is a recurrent figure.
She has a beak
and she can crack small things.
She has an eye
for lateral moments.
There are facts
that blur the line
between
the garden and the natural world.
And there are crows. They
lift off from the limbs
in the orange grove out back
and under cover of that sweet air
they land like WW II bombers
inside the garden.
Inside we wait for hunger.
Outside we wait for movement.
We want what is inside to go away.
We want what is outside
to be prey. On this morning,
fortune is with us.
The crows won't even play
on this turf.
There is big work
in other parts.
And wren
has a throat
reserved for cricket
and song.
It is cricket and song
that lead her
under moonlight
over stone.

An old wren with one good eye
is perched at the foot
of the statue of Pascal
rummaging and disheartened
but only for the moment.
Pascal throws a shadow,
long and dark
but the sun finds a way
between the stone toes,
the cracks in stone fabric.
Wren stalks a cricket now,
sees a bright future.

Wren is invisible
as anyone can see
and without being seen
she finds what she seeks.

When her form
leaves her shadow behind
she starts thinking
of nothing
and follows its flight.

From that height
and that distance
she locates a witness
who does the watching
over her
while she dreams
of going home.

But she never remembers
her dreams.

Within the canopy
of the hinoki cypress
two wrens,
friends for life,
in profile against
an early snow.
One enjoys a lichee nut
from somewhere.
The other watches
in silence.

Wren has trouble breathing
and nods for just seconds at a time.
Just as she falls into sleep
air backs up and she starts.
She thinks back
to moments of song
on wire and branch
before she ever noticed
cracks in the wind,
black dots in the field.

In a smoky daybreak,
she finds herself
motionless in a pepper tree
with the first few notes
about to burst.

She watches.
The red sun climbs.
She waits for a sign.

The color of red
the nature of risk
the noise of movement
the shape of night travel
changing by the moment
so as not to draw the attention
of those who would make us disappear
like an interruption in the wellspring
of dysphonia
which bursts from our throats.
Our head and body barely separated
by that throat.
No delay between dream and motion.
The dawn is red, there is red
between action and light.
Correct speed is required in this air
that is never still.
We are brown,
we are in a dangerous neighborhood,
we are not reckless
but we have gone in alone.
We will tell you the truth
we won't turn away
we won't fake the passion.
Red is that complicated.

Two wrens who look
extraordinarily alike
meet in a bell tower
in Puerto Rico.
Those bells haven't rung
for years
but if you think
the place is without music,
you're wrong.
Some old blackbirds
are going blind up there.

She follows the coastline
string on a picnic table.
She circles familiar wood
for days trying to find you.
She arrives above housetops
where you had been
just before
she came into view.

In the sky
there is the scent of you
everywhere.

The wild Mexican wrens gather
out beyond Temecula and
if there is peach cobbler involved
they break into improvisation
that will turn some heads.
The highs pierce the sky.
The wrens break down the
gates of themselves until
they nearly howl.
Anything with a mouth can
do some damage
if the sky stays big enough.

(for Art Pepper, 11-27-98, Aguanga & Rosarito)

This is not a question I want to ask
out loud but
why does no one recognize me?
I am in the ceilings at the Louvre
in the skies above the hunt
always flying near the king:
Le Roi et le roitelet.

And even three centuries later
there are the roofs
by Pont Neuf
and the cafes- that's a banquet.
The greasy pigeons take the best though-
where the storm drains empty, where that water
finds the river.
It's no longer clear where I belong.
In a $200 hotel I can't open a window.
And besides,
isn't le roitelet the spoiled French one
who only thinks
of California?

The North Atlantic seems moody tonight
and it rolls
between me and you.

In China, Wren is known
as the trickster who stole the crown
and headed for the Himalayas.
Wren was finally ambushed up there,
torn apart by messengers
of questionable affiliation.
And it made sense to Wren.
Now and then
assassination will carry off a bird
who would be King.

An estate near Philadelphia
A pair of Carolina Wrens
enter the sitting room
through a window
left partly open.
They build their nest
in the back of an upholstered sofa,
coming and going
through a hole torn in the cover.
They are not disturbed
and retain quiet possession
until the young are reared.

On the porch of the same house,
a brood in a rolled up
Japanese screen:

dawn after the great eclipse,
soldiers are hacking the wings
off a fiery mythic beast,
blood on snowy peaks
silver curved blade
unseen moon in tears
red silk
pale sky.

(In part, a found poem. The Carolina Wren,
National Audubon Society Leaflet No. 50
by Witmen Stone)

Night dwelling wren
dark in the glow
of the night-blooming cereus
and dwarfed by its casket-like
chutes.
The promise of dawn
the inevitability of real light
still far ahead
in the heat seeking
unquestioned
sometimes free of gravity
future.

(for Mai Hsu)

(for Mama Smith)

To avoid the tragedy
of inconsequence
two wrens are perched
on the lip of a dumpster
looking for something that shines.

The warm wind is pushy,
it's the brightest night of the year,
the moon is fat with itself
so everything shines.

Treasure is everywhere.

the wren
the sleeping rose
the vertical ascent
of a wounded bird.

Snake bait on the equator
on the edge of something.
If I can only find
St. Francis,
even a replica,
I'll climb up into those loving arms
and let them make me into wood
so I can sit safe and carved
in the bluest of night.

At Le Marché aux Oiseaux
two perfectly normal wrens,
Yvonne and Andre,
in a cage huddled together
in a Paris winter.
We smuggle them onto the liner
to keep us company.
It's February, 1951;
the North Atlantic
tosses the ship
like a stick.
Yvonne and Andre
are too shaken and cold to think,
they fall to the floor of the cage,
feet numb and up like a sundial.
The ship's doctor administers brandy
from a syringe.
Passengers gather,
eager for balance,
fresh from skeet shooting
and shuffleboard,
tempting small
miracles on the high seas.
In a minute,
Yvonne and Andre are up
and swaying to "La Vie En Rose,"
cutting through to the new world,
no stopovers.

I finally saw the Sign of the Wren
between my son's eyes it was
on the day
of the blue jay audition.

We looked at each other
and thought, this will never end.
But now we've learned to enjoy
the commotion
and we look forward to it
each year
measuring out time
by that splendid chaos.

(for my son, Saunder)

Constant the wren,
a slow thinker,
actually a fast thinker,
well,
busy,
this way and that,
but mostly on the surface
of things,
thorough,
yes,
but just on the surface.

Dawn takes me by surprise
but I'm always ready.
Dawn is not quiet
it is busy with relief.
I'd rather die in the light
I'd become blue neon
and take off in sequence (images)
stroking toward the dusk
futuristic
a gradual ascent
at 4 second intervals.
But I'm attached to some kind of
steel grid
so I cannot define gravity.
I try to take off through a
door, left open to prevent scandal
but the steel holds me,
keeps me in these places
that electricity permits.

In that cool blue/against/orange
it is the buzzing that keep me
going.

The morning air bursts
with bird conversation
dialogue and incantation
debate and invitation.
Wren is drunk with company
and sudden purpose.
Next door,
in a cottonwood,
a mockingbird
becomes a cell phone
ringing in the wild.

it is flat,
a surface to avoid
a surface far from home:

ice made beautiful
by fracture
by the brutal wind.

the early light,
hard and pale,
light without pity.

overhanging branches
throw lines, phantom limbs,
across the frozen flat.

wren circles twice,
sometimes too noisy
even to hear herself,
she finds a branch,
faces south,
puts a name
on this nameless place.

Fly over the big river
just for fun.
Take in your reflection.

Know the desert and
know the flight patterns
in that edgy space.
Don't land where
you're not wanted,
don't land where
 you are
wanted.
Land near the eggs
near warm feathers
that bind you to later.
And don't land too long.
Most of this landscape
will forget you
in a second.

I fly to keep from
staying still.
For me, it's fear
and crumbs.

In the sky
after I pass
there is no trace.

What could this flight
possibly be
about?

I always wanted
to hold still
long enough
for you.

(for daughter, Leslie)

ghost wren
dreaming on a cable
posed
and still
like a shadow
about to dart
into a windless space
flesh and fiber
anticipating
the tension of wound steel
a cello in the night
an ordinary cello
still
in a windless room

Wren is surrounded
by madness and treachery
boxed in by promises
broken like shale
like the shell
of an unlucky mollusk
dropped onto rock
by the gulls
she has always despised.

Wren did not know how to forage,
"Why don't these poets get to the point?"
she asked.
Wren went nearly crazy until
she learned to fly.

By April,
Wren was a nervous wreck.
"Why does this wind shift
so suddenly, why can't
these updrafts lay flat?"
she asked.
When the council of birds laughed as one,
she regurgitated barleycorn
and leg of violin spider.

Swallows peal off from the front
of the formation to draft at
the back.
Air passes through Wren
without a trace.
"Are we there yet?"
she asks.

Wired together by rain
and thunder
by a song we barely remember,

2 wrens on a chain link fence
in rain
and cold
dorsal feathers shining
in winter light.

From a roof
you can sometimes tell
what will happen next
to something sitting on a fence.

When the sun comes round again
there is an empty chain link fence.

Wren, always drawn to small pictures,
beads of nectar on a wire
a june bug, a seed
from the eye of a sunflower
fallen in black soil.

Wren knows
when you hunt like the jackal
you find answers.

Inside the grille
of a Buick Le Sabre
just in from Phoenix
a cactus wren
picks a rare hot meal
off a cooling radiator.

She looks up and watches
crows from a different neighborhood
shake down a red-tailed hawk,
run her right out of view.

Such a tiny skeleton,
the structure,
an island
moving on air,
here and there.
Small messages
floating ashore.

Then, a palm tree,
a breathless hideaway.
A place to wait for silence,
a palm tree
with dusk deepening.
A place to learn
to be brown.

Wren wears herself out
in the darkness of these trees.

How she stays alive
is nobody's business.

Three wrens
drifting like orphans,
pictured on the wall of a cave.
You have to look closely
among the crows and eagles.
Wren on a branch
by the burial ground;
wren, a dot or a dash
in a telegraphic sky;
wren lakeside
at the summit
of an imperfect dawn.

Brother crow turned black
putting out fires
on Acoma land.
Wren turned brown
greeting a dusty sky;
the earth itself
whirls
and sings a crooked song.

Miscalculating a landing,
in a shaft
of uneasy updraft,
wren winds up too tight,
breaks a beak
bangs against
unforgiving rock.

Wren had a lot of time to think
back then;
she grew fat
in the olive trees
while she mended.

That's why she was still in Jerusalem
when Jesus died on Calvary.
And she saw it all:
when a woman came out of the crowd
to swab his bloody face
with her veil,
when a man came out of the crowd
to help hoist the timber.

And a shadow
passed over wren

At the Sixth Station
she sat and wondered,

as she often does,
"what would it be like
to serve in an extreme way?"
What would fuel her?
Fear, rapture, guilt or grace?

After two days
she saw the crows
at their work
and she knew.

We have never lived
in a land without the wren.
That's why we shake and tremble
until the wind becomes home,
becomes the sky
we fly
into.

(thanks to Jimmy Coen)

It's not really fear:
the sound of waves
rolling and erasing,
scrubbing the sand,
making it tumble,

rock and pebble to sand
over and over.

She neither fears nor trusts
the sound. She is
just a wren headed north
but she knows that sound
was made by a master
if ever there was
such a thing.

Do masters come and go
like the waves,
she wonders.

And as for heading north,
it just means leaving a place
for the last time,
arriving, always arriving,
and for the last time.
What she leaves,
she leaves forever.

What remains
will also vanish

and look the same

like leaving
as you arrive.

a broken wren
in a cardboard box
and I will teach it to fly
wren in a jail cell
giving a man new life
wren in a military zone
sweetly unaware
new to this brand of death
true to the song
free in space
bursting in air
breaking up into
the indifferent sea

The first kiss,
two wrens on fire,
blind with smoke and heat
storming out of the underbrush
of self-restraint
into a trembling
orgasmic future
well above the starving dogs,
fast food chains,
the quick fixes below.
This flame will lick the wound.
This flame will light up like this.
This flame will consume.

On the 17th floor of the Flatiron Bldg., two
high powered Bushnell lenses are trained on our
little park. I can't imagine what the attraction
might be. Anyway, when we sing like this,
we are connected to all of history. The first
Monarch of the season will teach us to hit the
knuckleball. And on the 17th floor of the
Flatiron Bldg., an 89 year old woman, who
no longer speaks, is pressed against the glass.
Now I know she was always watching over me.

You can transfer to Yankee Stadium right here at
Madison Square. They raise a lot of racket up
there. Today, we belong in the noise.

(for Dorothy)

| Rick Smith

Something dangerous,
a red-tailed hawk
and coming fast,
like wind
off Lake Michigan.

Wren, lost in dreams,
freezes, off-guard.

The hawk
snaps a yard rat
off a clothesline
not ten feet away.

Motionlessness
disguises anxiety.

Wren breaks out
of dream time,
arguing with unruly ghosts.

a scattering of wrens,
a familiar but
transient reed section
working without charts.

dumbfounding,
they go about business
with single-minded intent.

these two nest in the eye socket
of the steer skull
by a wooden door

between winds,
between the scattering,
enthused packets
of breath and mission

don't ask how I know.

Bonnie Love-Nordoff

The high fever pitch
of dry lightning
shakes the only tree for miles.
The breath of a devil wind,
the ink filled sky…
Some suitcase farmer
trying to hit a crop
waits for a train
out of the Panhandle
where the dust is thick,
where the wind is King.

Wren can't see a thing,
the wheat,
stacked high,
rots in heaps.

Wren blows south,
then west,
has a run in
with a barbed wire fence.

Wren is selfless
in a North Texas night.

in certain light,
nature makes her a screamer,
a pissed and troubled
puddle of a bird
who cannot locate a reflection
on any surface

as the smallest wren,
screaming like the fire
that runs through her frame,
flies out of the sunrise
like a savage
with rage so haunting,
her exhaustion
turns to fuel

now there is a pond
close below her,
always close

behind an orange drink sign
on the highway
where you are

picture me
as something you might have missed,
a common pebble, a ground squirrel,
the kind of neighbor who moves
every time the rent comes due.

always picture me near the music
and the dance,
right where life begins,
in a sky of China Blue
and always in the vicinity
of planet earth.

(for Sharon West)

near Biloxi:
a shotgun house

the rains
muddy and cold

window frames
slam and shatter

someone steals a boat
paddles east

a dog stranded
on a roof

a wren finds a nail
under the eaves

the wind
shredding anything that moves
drowns out
all other sound

now:
two wrens
on a nail
dream
against the storm

The caribou won't believe it
until humility no longer matters.
He is undaunted by any
Yukon Pacific chemin de fer
wandering all jerky and loud
hauling lumber or oil
through his private outback,
like a common pack mule
working for oats.

And so he stands his ground
confident and in no hurry.
(this smoke spitting piece of junk metal
isn't shrewd like brother wolf
who comes with running buddies
and a plan.)
The noise, though,
the howl and rhythm,
does reach an impressive din
and that tiny head
behind a black window,
a suddenly blazing light...
and everything gets huge.

The recognition of possibilities
crosses his mind
in dead heat
with his flank.

9000 feet high in The Little Belt Mountains
(he didn't get there by himself),
Wren watches a caribou
hit by an American made engine.
Wren does nothing,
can do nothing
to prevent the kill.
Caribou never listened to any word from Wren.
They didn't have that kind
of relationship.

Snowy boxcars
rumble by,
clicking and clacking.
Nothing
ever happened.

A grey wren
foolish enough
to believe in indian summer
stares into a black
and gritty wind
shakes with every gust,
imagines a subtle hand
on a dimmer switch
in a night
slow descending.

When wren is absent
where does she go?

Messenger wren
off on a mission
but lost in dense fog
over tangled mountain trails
where no one travels.
The lungs burn,
the air too thin,
too rare.

The message is code.
Wren is not sure
whose side she's on.
She only knows it's cold,
hard to think.
She's not cut out
for running errands.

When she finds her way
to the flat land
she picks up a twig,
forgets to put it down.

It's a hard land
and too much bad water
makes her dizzy.

Wren cannot grow fat
or careless.

She stands in air
looks in all directions at once
before dropping
into the sound
of touchdown.

She imagines heights,
clouds,
faraway stars
but finds the chain link
and rowhouse rooftops
of North Phillie.

Wren lives a small life
in a hard land.

She imagines heights,
drinks bad water.

She recognizes danger.
she can't land.
she can't shake off fear
like pond water
anymore.

The sweep
of a terrible wingspan,
a brush stroke
sways bulrushes
on a distant bank.

This is how poison is made:
by squeezing drops of terror
out of wren,
draining the pulse,
the tears
with a curved silver beak.

The greedy talons
may release her
but she'll never be the same.

She shares two shores,
and two small deaths.

She can
no longer depend
on this world.

(Nearly any bird
will avoid a tree
lit by torches;
the fear of human ritual
is deeply woven.)

If wren watches anything
too long
she's afraid to look away.
Sometimes she can see
clear through
to stone and silt.

Engaged in gazing
at nothing
she spots something red
by the river.

Something red
could distract her
make her change direction.
She'd rather gaze at nothing,
the thin line
that divides the invisible
and the nonexistent.

At Puerto Nuevo,
wren watches
while a western grebe
slices into a rough surface,
comes up with a still struggling meal,
new to flight.

Wren cannot make a dent
in any water
but she sees
all she dreams
on the outskirts
of this town
in a puddle
upside
down.

Back in 86 A.D.,
I think it was about that time
as people count it.
For me, it's just a distant blue.
Sometimes these stories are passed down
and they replace actual memory.

It was decided
back then:
each flock would send their best
to touch the sky
with the highest flier
crowned.
I wasn't around when they dreamed this up.
I would have been against it
but that's wind under a branch.
I want to tempt memory,
the memory of that flight, because
I'm not a liar but I'm willing to lie
and somewhere in that memory is what I've lost
and what I was.
When I imagined trying to outdo the eagle
or the hawk, I thought, why bother?
I'll just be smeared and forgotten in
the lower atmosphere, wheezing
and feeling my breast catch fire.

Ok, lets start from the beginning.
I had a dream that I was king.
Is that really a crime? No, it's not.
But between me and that dream
was the eagle and his crowd.
Can you really blame me?
If you read the fine print,
it says, "the one who reaches the highest point."

So what if I let the eagle do all the work?
She never really knew

I was there,
a stowaway in thinning air.
I took off fresh at 12,000 feet
and picked up another ten yards.
The real miracle
is how I ever got back down.
It's freezing up there
and I never could catch the wind
like that raptorial clan.
It's far higher than I've ever been.
I don't have that kind of structure.
The free fall nearly narced me out.
My wings and eyes didn't want to work.
I always thought it was supposed to be warm
up there, close to the sun and all,
but it's the opposite.
I started thawing out at 600 feet
and wobbled in from there.
I felt blessed to be back on the limb of a juniper,
30 feet up, but there was
more than a murmur of discontent from the assembled
and I had to use my craft
to get out of there in one piece.
Keep moving.
That's something I learned on the desert floor.
I kept thinking
this dream feels pretty real
and it turns out, it was.

In the dream I became king.
But not in every sector.
It actually started a riot.
I became a target over here,
died a figurehead over there.
I was minted and thrived,
then hunted and despised.
Don't worry though, I'm over it.
I made my mark, at least in Europe.

In Asia they deconstructed me, In
North America, I'm invisible. The eagle has
these territories mesmerized.

No one talks about South America much.
Terra Incognito.
Africa, the same.
Titles don't mean a thing there.
Besides,
the meat-eating vegetation,
the green mamba
watching for a careless landing,
the uncompromising blackness
and movement of night
make those places unthinkable.
But in Europe I'm everywhere.
On stamps and coins
and scored deep into the very
music of the language.

The dream is the best way to retrieve something buried
in tissue, buried in prehistory. There's a distance and still
there's a now there. Things past, things yet to pass, things
elusive but destined to be. Beginnings seeking the now.

I took a breath, I aimed high.
I pushed off and marked a spot
for better or for worse. I held the note
long and rich as I could.
So what if it's the only note I know?
It's my note.

I don't wear the mask of the hawk;
I'm too tiny
to have caused this much stir.
Too anonymous.
And yet I find no peace.
Even my internal workings rebel, wind up, explode,

drive me out into the wilderness,
drive me to exhaust myself.
And when sleep finally comes
I have this dream.
The pictures flow back to me
in black formation. Back when
it started, there was color,
cherry red, the orange and gold
of the Fauves,
but now, always in black.

That's because I have certain knowledge
that draws the color out:
Black water, black air, black light,
black and quiet acres.

Eagle came once to talk.
The rain was furious.
"I'll never let it go," she said,
and picked a tuft of something
off her glacier-like frame,
"I can still feel your pulse
in the upper atmosphere.
Your pulse, draining me
in small ways."

There will be
no melting
of this
ancient ice.

Now I'm told,
"the real ones fly alone."
Like I care.

They're always making up new rules
to make me look like a pretender.
It's bad enough living without color,

but always scanning the horizon,
the top soil, the lower branches...

I'm learning to play by my own rules,
to make no excuses,
to have less fear.
It hasn't always been this way
but eventually you have to say
what have I got to lose?
That's when I stopped
I shook loose and headed for open space,
without a past,
nothing to look back at.
Forgetting gives us a fresh start
and passage into a clean and perfect present
or maybe into a stiff cold wind where we
fly with angels.

We seek silence and peace
and fly with angels,
not really alone,
with angels.

In celebration of St. Stephen's Day,
Wren is hung by the legs.
The Wren Boys wander through Dublin
chanting and holding a mobile
of dead wrens.

The wren is tiny
like the red still fist
of a sleeping child.

Wren comes back as The Holy Bull.

About Rick Smith >>>

Raised in Manhattan, Paris, Toledo, Ohio, and Bucks County, Pennsylvania. Rick Smith began writing under the guidance of Michael Casey at Solebury School in Pennsylvania. Close family friendships and Carl Sandburg and Lenore Marshall also made a lasting impact on Rick's life choices. He went on to study with Anthony Hecht at Bard College, George Starbuck, Marvin Bell and Frank Polite at the University of Iowa and Sam Eisenstein at Los Angeles City College. He learned blues harmonica in the "basket houses" of Greenwich Village and in the roadhouses of Duchess County. Smith founded the City Lights on the Sunset Strip in 1965 and has played and recorded with the likes of Van Dyke Parks, Big Joe Williams, Bernie Perl, Clabe Hangan and Steve Mann. During the 70's, he joined Dan Ilves to co-edit the literary journal, Stonecloud. In 1981, he and John Lyon wrote and recorded "Hand To Mouth" a well reviewed LP of originals. He went on to write and record with Mindless, Go Figure, The Hangan Brothers and The Mescal Sheiks. Smith continues to work with the Mescal Sheiks as well as with Music Formula. He is a clinical psychologist, in Rancho Cucamonga, California where he specializes in brain damage and domestic violence; he spent several years on the internationally acclaimed neurological service allied health team at Rancho Los Amigos Medical Center in Downey, California. He and his wife, Erika, have a 16 year old son, Saunder; Rick also has adult daughters, Leslie and Ruby, and granddaughters Dylon, Truth, and Ava. Rick Smith is published widely in anthologies and in small press publications such as New Letters, Onthebus, Blueline, Hanging Loose, Pinyon, Eclipse, Paper Street, Lummox, Rattle, Rhino and Main Street Rag...

Also by Rick Smith >>>

Poetry
Exhibition Game *(G. Sack Press, 1973)*
The Wren Notebook *(Lummox Press, 2000)*

Recordings
The City Lights: On The Road Again *(Cadet. 1966; 45 rpm)*
Fat City Jug Band *(Custom Fidelity, 1969; lp)*
Chuck Bridges: L.A. Happening *(Vault Records, 1970; lp)*
The Rick Smith Band: Hand to Mouth *(Deep Dish, 1981; lp)*
Mindless: Riddim & Blooz *(Rockin' House, 1991; cassette)*
The Hangan Brothers: Life Is a Hard Blues *(Deep Water, 1997; cd)*
                     Mars Market *(Blue Cap, 2000; cd)*
Larry Jackson: Believe It Or Not *(Far West Mississippi Recordings, 1999; cd)*
The Mescal Sheiks: This World Is Not My Home *(Blue Cap, 2003; cd)*
Ernest Troost: Resurrection Blues *(Travelin' Shoes Music, 2009; cd)*

Soundtracks
Days of Heaven *(Paramount, 1976)*
Baby Luv *(Mojave Films, 1999)*
Vigilantette *(Lyon Hart Films, 2004)*

Producer (with John Lyon)
Steve Mann Live At The Ash Grove *(Half Blind's Choice, 1975; lp*
                     and Bella Roma Music, 2008; cd)

Anthologies
Foreign Exchange, a clack of American poets *(Biographics, 1979)*
The Aspect 10 Year Anthology *(Zephyr Press, 1981)*
Eyes Like Mingus *(Lummox Press, 1999)*
Lost Highway *(Lummox Press, 2002)*
So Luminous The Wildflowers *(Tebot Bach, 2003)*
Familiar *(The People's Press, 2005)*
Hunger Enough *(Puddinghouse Publications, 2005)*
a chaos of angels *(Word Walker, 2006)*
The Long Way Home *(Lummox Press, 2009)*
Reeds and Rushes *(Puddinghouse Publications, 2010)*

ABOUT THE LUMMOX PRESS ›››

Lummox Press was created in 1994 by RD Armstrong. It began as a self-publishing/DIY imprint for poetry by RD. Several chapbooks were published and in late 1995 it began publishing the **Lummox Journal**, a monthly small/underground press lit-arts zine. Available primarily by subscription, the LJ continued its exploration of the "creative process" until its demise as a print mag in 2006.

During its eleven year existence, this tiny mag with the big name interviewed poets, musicians and artists (over 100 in all) about how they do what they do. Hundreds of poems were also published in its pages. Poets like *Todd Moore, Lyn Lifshin, Gerald Locklin, Holly Prado, L.A. Bogen, Linda Lerner, Scott Wannberg, Philomene Long, John Thomas* and *RD Armstrong*, to name a few, appeared regularly within its pages. It was hailed as one of the best monthlies in the small press.

In 1998, Lummox began publishing the **Little Red Book** series, and continues to do so today. To date (as of 2010) there are some 59 titles in the series and a collection of poems from the first decade of the series has been published under the title, **The Long Way Home** (2009).

Lummox also publishes limited edition books such as **The Wren Notebook** by Rick Smith (2000) and **Last Call: The Legacy of Charles Bukowski** (2004). More recently, Lummox published a set of four titles from its founder, RD Armstrong: **On/Off the Beaten Path** (a trio of long poems about road trips taken in 1999, 2000 and 2001 including the epic poem **RoadKill** – which John Berbrich said was "the best post 9-11 writing I've seen"), **Fire and Rain – Selected Poems 1993-2007** Volumes **1 & 2** and **El Pagano and Other Twisted Tales** (a collection of short stories and flash fiction). All were published in 2008.

In late 2008 Lummox began publishing the **RESPECT** series starting with **John Yamrus'** <u>**New and Selected Poems**</u>. This was followed by **Todd Moore**'s <u>**The Riddle of the Wooden Gun**</u> (2009); <u>**Sea Trails**</u> by **Pris Campbell** (2009) and <u>**Down This Crooked Road – Modern Poetry from the Road Less Traveled**</u> edited by **RD Armstrong** and **William Taylor, Jr.** (2009). In 2010, **John Bennett's** <u>**Drive By – Shards and Poems**</u> was followed by <u>**Modest Aspirations – Poems & Stories**</u> by **Gerald Locklin & Beth Wilson;** <u>**Steel Valley**</u> by **Michael Adams** followed. These books are available directly from the Lummox Press via the website: **www.lummoxpress.com** or at **Lummox** c/o PO Box 5301 San Pedro, CA 90733. There are also E-Book versions of most titles available. The RESPECT series, as well as RD's four titles are also available on line.

Please visit the website to read selections from these titles as well as peruse the many other titles/articles published by the Lummox Press.

Ask your independent bookstore to carry these titles, since Lummox only deals with independent book stores like Powell's of Portland, OR; The Book Collector of Sacramento, CA or Moe's of Berkeley, CA.

Together with Chris Yeseta (Layout and Art Direction since 1997), RD continues to publish books that are both striking in their looks as well as their content...you'd think he was aping *Black Sparrow*, but he is merely trying to produce the best books he can for his clients, the poets, and their customers, you, the readers.

CONTACT:
poetraindog@gmail.com
www.lummoxpress.com

www.ingramcontent.com/pod-product-compliance
Lightning Source LLC
Chambersburg PA
CBHW020921090426
42736CB00008B/738